First Facts®

Ice Age Animals

the BIG PICTURE

CAPSTONE PRESS
a capstone imprint

Louise Spilsbury

First Facts is published by Capstone Press, a Capstone imprint,
151 Good Counsel Drive, P.O. Box 669, Mankato, Minnesota 56002.
www.capstonepub.com

First published in 2010 by A&C Black Publishers Limited, 36 Soho Square, London W1D 3QY
www.acblack.com
Copyright © A&C Black Ltd. 2010

Produced for A&C Black by Calcium. www.calciumcreative.co.uk

032010
005746ACF10

Library of Congress Cataloging-in-Publication Data
Spilsbury, Louise.
  Ice Age Animals / by Louise Spilsbury.
    p. cm. — (First facts, the big picture)
  Includes bibliographical references and index.
  ISBN 978-1-4296-5508-8 (library binding)
  ISBN 978-1-4296-5518-7 (paperback)
 1. Extinction (Biology)—Juvenile literature. 2. Glacial
epoch—Juvenile literature. I. Title. II. Series.

  QE721.2.E97S68 2011
  560'.1792—dc22   2010012856

Every effort has been made to trace copyright holders and to obtain their permission for use of copyright material.

This book is produced using paper that is made from wood grown in managed, sustainable forests. It is natural,
renewable and recyclable. The logging and manufacturing processes conform to the environmental regulations
of the country of origin.

Acknowledgements

The publishers would like to thank the following for their kind permission to reproduce their photographs:

Cover: Shutterstock: Murray Lundberg (front), Ozja (back). **Pages:** Alamy Images: David Crausby 6-7; Corbis:
Sergei Cherkashin/Reuters 21; Fotolia: Michal Lindner 8, Marc Strauch 10-11; Istockphoto: Jens Klingebiel 18-19,
Jacynth Roode 4-5; Science Photo Library: Christian Darkin 1, 9; Shutterstock: BBBB 16-17, Blucie Photo 12-13,
Boris Bort 24, Mike Brake 2-3, Elena Galach'yants 14-15, Ralf Juergen Kraft 14-15, 18, Michael Ledray 3, 20,
Murray Lundberg 16, Carsten Medom Madsen 17, Nialat 10, Tyler Olson 6-7, 8-9, 20-21, Ozja 12,
Ian Scott 4-5, Alexey Stiop 22-23.

Contents

Ice Age

A long time ago, the Earth was covered in snow and ice. This time was called the Ice Age.

Amazing animals

Strange animals lived in the Ice Age. There were tigers with giant teeth and amazing elephants with long hair!

Megalodon was an Ice Age shark. It was bigger than a great white shark!

Too cold

It was so cold in the Ice Age that some animals could not survive. They died out. Megalodon was a giant shark that died out when oceans froze during the Ice Age.

Super shark!

Land of Giants

Large animals keep warm more easily than small ones, so many Ice Age animals were giants!

Don't mess with me!

The glyptodont was a huge **armadillo** that was as big as a car. It had a tough shell to protect it from other animals that might try to eat it.

The ground sloth was as big as a jeep!

Super sloth

The ground sloth could stand on its back legs and had claws as long as a man's forearm!

Giant claws

Hairy Monsters

Some Ice Age animals had lots of long, shaggy hair to keep them warm.

Furry elephants?

Woolly mammoths had a coat of long hair to keep them warm. They even had fur inside their ears!

Woolly mammoths looked like hairy elephants!

Woolly rhinos

Woolly rhinos may have used their **horns** and **tusks** to scrape away snow to eat plants beneath.

Bad hair day!

9

In Hiding

Many Ice Age animals had white fur to blend in with the snow.

Hunt or hide

Many Ice Age animals had white fur so they could hide from **predators** or sneak up on **prey**.

Snowshoe hares are still around today.

You can't see me!

Going white

The polar bear was once brown! It slowly turned white during the Ice Age to blend in with the snow.

Killer Cats

Cats that lived in the Ice Age were not the cuddly kind!

Heavyweight hunter

Saber-toothed tigers were as big as a lion but twice as heavy. They pinned down their prey and killed it with their huge, deadly teeth.

The saber-toothed tiger was bigger and fiercer than tigers are today.

Saw and slice

The scimitar cat was as big as the saber-toothed tiger. Its teeth had **jagged** edges like a saw— for slicing up animals!

Meeooooow!

Fierce Fighters

If you had been alive in the Ice Age you would have had to watch out for fierce hunters!

Biggest killer

Andrewsarchus was the biggest meat-eater to ever live on land. It was like a huge dog with **hooves** and powerful jaws and teeth.

Wooof!

Hungry wolves

Dire wolves were only a little bigger than a gray wolf, but their teeth were huge! They worked in **packs** to bring down large prey.

Andrewsarchus was as tall as three men!

Ice Age People

People found ways to survive the cold and to stay alive in the Ice Age.

Making a home

People built homes from mammoth bones or branches covered with animal skin. They also kept warm by making clothes from animal skin.

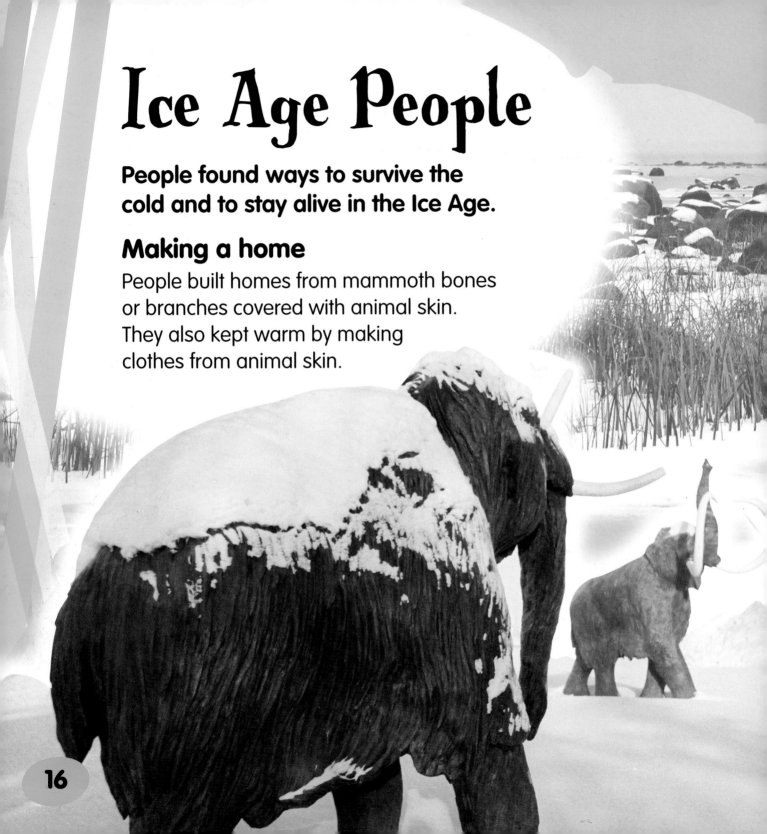

Finding food

Ice Age people hunted mammoths and fish. They also ate berries and plants. They cooked food on fires, and buried it in the snow to keep it fresh.

People made tools from stone for cutting plants and meat.

17

Gone Forever

When the Ice Age ended, the weather became warmer and wetter. Many Ice Age animals then died out.

Nothing to eat

As the ice melted, water covered the land where animals **grazed**. Plant-eaters like the mammoth may have starved to death.

With less prey to eat, meat-eaters such as Andrewsarchus died.

Still alive

Some Ice Age animals are still alive today. **Musk oxen** lived in North America during the Ice Age. They can still be found in very cold places.

How We Know

We know about Ice Age animals because of fossils. These are the parts of dead things that are left behind, such as bones, teeth, and tusks.

Piecing it together

Scientists piece fossils together to find out how Ice Age animals may have looked.

Scary fossil!

20

Frozen forever

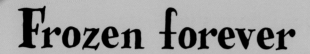

Some places have stayed covered in ice since the Ice Age. Here people have found frozen woolly mammoths and woolly rhinos.

This baby mammoth was found in the ice.

Glossary

armadillo animal with a hard, bony shell

graze to eat grass and other plants

hooves hard coverings on some animals' feet

horns hard spikes on top of an animal's head

jagged rough and sharp

musk oxen animal a little like a cow, but covered in lots of warm, woolly hair

packs groups of animals

predators an animal that hunts other animals for food

prey animal that is eaten by another animal for food

tusks hard spikes on an animal's face

Further Reading

FactHound offers a safe, fun way to find Internet sites related to this book. All of the sites on FactHound have been researched by our staff.

Here's all you do:

Visit www.facthound.com

FactHound will fetch the best sites for you!

Books

You Wouldn't Want to be a Mammoth Hunter! (Dangerous Beasts You'd Rather Not Encounter) by John Malam, Franklin Watts (2004).

In the Ice Age (Andrew Lost) by J.C. Greenburg, Random House Books (2005).

Ice Age Sabertooth: The Most Ferocious Cat That Ever Lived by Barbara Hehner, Crown Publishers (2002).

Index